T0195082

LEVELS
OF
TRUST

ALICIA HARPER

authorHOUSE®

AuthorHouse™
1663 Liberty Drive
Bloomington, IN 47403
www.authorhouse.com
Phone: 833-262-8899

Published by AuthorHouse   01/31/2022

ISBN: 978-1-6655-5059-8 (sc)
ISBN: 978-1-6655-5061-1 (e)

Library of Congress Control Number: 2022901838

Print information available on the last page.

DEDICATIONS

To My Family:

You have seen me at my lowest levels. You prayed me through. Intercession is a gift. Inside of it is power. I am the evidence of your belief in God and for who He is. I am the result of your trust in Him.

To My Husband:

You recognize God in me. You never allow me to give up. You encourage me every day to dig deeper. It causes me to fly higher. Thank you for loving and encouraging me through everyone of my processes. You are my God given blessing.

To The Reader:

Do it God's way! Embrace every level. The levels you have already been through and the level you're on now. Appreciate every new trusting for the levels to come!

"And I am certain that God, who began the good work within you, will continue his work until it is finally finished on the day when Christ Jesus returns."

Philippians 1:6

CONTENTS

Introduction ix

Level 1   Jesus Is Baptized 1

Level 2   Jesus Rides Into Jerusalem 6

Level 3   Jesus Prays 11

Level 4   Jesus Is Arrested 22

Level 5   Jesus Forgives 27

Level 6   Jesus Fights Abandonment 31

Level 7   Jesus Entrusts His Spirit 37

INTRODUCTION

Jesus traveled through levels of faith
confident in The Father. Abba Father.
God Who is Adonai, our Total Authority.
The Lord. He is El, The strong One.
He is Emmanuel, God with us. The
immeasurable 'I Am', the self-existent
One. He never changes and His promises
never fail. He is faithful. He is El Elyon,
The God Most High. The Sovereign God,
in Whom we can put our trust. We can
depend on Him. He is The Great Deliverer!

Jesus is the blueprint of how one is to commit. The foundation of how necessary it is to follow the instructions of God. Trusting, honoring and reverencing The Almighty One at every step in life.

This book begins with its concentration on Jesus and his last words on the cross. His final moment transitioning to his proper place, seated at the right hand of God. In Luke 23:46 in the New Living Translation it reads,

"Then Jesus shouted, "Father, I entrust my spirit into your hands!" And with those words he breathed his last."

In the King James Version it reads,

"And when Jesus had cried with a loud voice, he said, Father, into thy hands I commend my spirit: and having said thus, he gave up the ghost."

Jesus is the living example of working our way up to commending our whole life into God's mighty hands. In the NLT this verse uses the word "entrust". In the KJV "commend".

Entrust: Confidence to put trust on The Deliverer
Commend: To give for care or preservation officially.

IT'S LEVELS TO THIS!!!

Every Level holds another degree of entrusting. A new commending. Another trust to put on. A fresh confidence. Officially addressing the next!

Strap in! We're about to travel through Jesus' seven levels of trust. Using them as a guideline, as well as encouragement, to journey through our own levels. Going from faith to faith and glory to Glory.

LEVEL 1

Jesus Is Baptized

Water baptism is done when one has a repentive heart and a change of mind. A desire to turn from a previous lifestyle of sin. It's a desired longing to wash away their old man. To become a new. It requires something before you even get in!

Now Jesus had no sin. He had no need of repentance. So why did he get baptized?

Heaven is how earth is supposed to be. This baptism began the reconnection between God and man. The infusion of heaven released to us and over us.

Jesus is the example! Jesus went in already changed. Is your mind made up? Are you ready for change? When your mind is changed God can work with you.

Real went into the water when Jesus got in. The heavens were torn open and Fire came down, the Holy Spirit.

In Matthew 3:15 (NLT) when talking to John;

> "But Jesus said, "It should be
> done, for we must carry out
> all that God requires." So John
> agreed to baptize him."

John recognized Jesus as the Messiah but Jesus recognized God as the Creator and Author. He honored every direction of The Everlasting, Self Existent God.

Here he is committing himself to carrying out his assignment. He is equipped with the power of the Holy Spirit upon him.

LEVELS OF TRUST

God is well pleased. Jesus is prepared, filled with the Holy Spirit. And immediately he is led by The Spirit into the wilderness. This is the first level of testing. Yes there will be tests. Tested faith can be trusted. We can see this in Matthew 4:1-11 (NLT);

"Then Jesus was led by the Spirit into the wilderness to be tempted there by the devil. (2.) For forty days and forty nights he fasted and became very hungry. (3.) During that time the devil came and said to him, "If you are the Son of God, tell these stones to become loaves of bread." (4.) But Jesus told him, "No! The Scriptures say, 'People do not live by bread alone, but by every word that comes from the mouth of God.'" (5.) Then the devil took him to the holy city, Jerusalem, to the highest point of the Temple, (6.) and said, "If you are the Son of God, jump off! For the Scriptures say, 'He will order his angels to protect you. And they will hold you up with their hands so you won't even hurt your foot on a stone.'" (7.) Jesus responded, "The Scriptures also say, 'You must not test the LORD your God.'" (8.) Next the devil took him to the peak of a very high mountain and showed him all the kingdoms of the world and their glory. (9.)"I will give it all to you," he said, "if you will kneel down and worship me." (10.)"Get out of here, Satan," Jesus told him. "For the Scriptures say, 'You must worship the LORD your God and serve only him.'" (11.)Then the devil went away, and angels came and took care of Jesus."

Jesus combated temptation with The Word of God and prevailed!

LEVEL UP

NOTES

_____

_____

_____

_____

_____

_____

_____

_____

_____

_____

_____

_____

_____

_____

_____

_____

_____

_____

_____

_____

_____

LEVEL 2

Jesus Rides Into Jerusalem

Jesus wastes no time between His baptism and moving into His assigned calling.

He has taught on be-attitudes, salt and light. The law, anger, vows, revenge, prayer and fasting. The heart of giving, possessions as well as effective prayer, The Golden Rule and building on the solid foundation. Lastly, but most important, compassion and love.

He has healed the leopards and the lame. Calmed storms, opened blind eyes and created disciples. He has fed five-thousand, walked on water, prayed and delivered and raised the dead.

Jesus is breaking up the system! But he doesn't sneak into the city. He boldly rides in to meet his destiny, fulfilling the scripture. John 12:12-18 (NLT) reads;

> "The next day, the news that Jesus was on the way to Jerusalem swept through the city. A large crowd of Passover visitors (13.) took palm branches and went down the road to meet him. They shouted, "Praise God! Blessings on the one who comes in the name of the Lord! Hail to the King of Israel!" (14.) Jesus found a young donkey and rode on it, fulfilling the prophecy that said: (15.) "Don't be afraid, people of Jerusalem. Look, your King is coming, riding on a donkey's colt. (16.) His disciples

didn't understand at the time that this was a fulfillment of prophecy. But after Jesus entered into his glory, they remembered what had happened and realized that these things had been written about him. (17.) Many in the crowd had seen Jesus call Lazarus from the tomb, raising him from the dead, and they were telling others about it. (18.) That was the reason so many went out to meet him—because they had heard about this miraculous sign."

Jesus keeps going! He turns over tables in the temple, he challenges and criticizes the religious leaders and continues to teach God's people The Truth. He also begins to prepare his mind and his disciples for what is to come. The greater work.

Jesus knows he's getting closer. In John 12:27-28 (NLT) He says;

""Now my soul is deeply troubled. Should I pray, 'Father, save me from this hour'? But this is the very reason I came! (28.)Father, bring glory to your name." Then a voice spoke from heaven, saying, "I have already brought glory to my name, and I will do so again.""

He has resolved within himself that he has come too far to turn back. He acknowledges that his obedience holds a never ending ripple effect. An intentionally pervasive wave. Spreading through and existing in every part of mankind.

LEVEL UP

NOTES

_____

_____

_____

_____

_____

_____

_____

_____

_____

_____

_____

_____

_____

_____

_____

_____

_____

_____

_____

_____

_____

LEVEL 3

Jesus Prays

Signs, wonders and miracles follow Jesus. Many works were done where the people were open and receptive. Multiple works were done for all of those willing, ready and available to receive him. But the disciples were privileged to intimately walk with him. Through this journey they bore witness to the significance of his prayer life.

The disciples asked him, "Jesus how did you heal the sick and we couldn't?" He responded,

"Prayer and fasting". But they never asked, "How did you raise the dead?" They understood the power of his communication with The Father. Prayer or communication equates to a relationship. This relationship results in power! They asked him to teach them how to pray. We find this in Luke 11:1-4 (NLT);

> "Once Jesus was in a certain
> place praying. As he finished,
> one of his disciples came to
> him and said, "Lord, teach us
> to pray, just as John taught
> his disciples." (2.) Jesus said,
> "This is how you should pray:
> "Father, may your name be kept
> holy. May your Kingdom come
> soon. (3.) Give us each day the
> food we need, (4.) and forgive
> us our sins, as we forgive those
> who sin against us. And don't
> let us yield to temptation.""

They caught on to the connection between Jesus' power and his lifestyle of prayer. When asked to share this essential key, that was his immediate response. He freely gave what had been given to him. We must do the same. He also went further in Luke 11:9-13 (NLT);

> ""And so I tell you, keep on asking, and you will receive what you ask for. Keep on seeking, and you will find. Keep on knocking, and the door will be opened to you. (10.) For everyone who asks, receives. Everyone who seeks, finds. And to everyone who knocks, the door will be opened. (11.) "You fathers—if your children ask for a fish, do you give them a snake instead? (12.) Or if they ask for an egg, do you give them a scorpion? Of course not! (13.) So if you sinful people know how to give good gifts to your children, how much more will your heavenly Father give the Holy Spirit to those who ask him.""

This approach to prayer acknowledges:

1. God as our Father.
2. God The Holy One. King of kings and Lord of lords.
3. God's will is to be done. Here with us as it is in Heaven.

This approach to prayer, with acknowledgement to who God is, teaches the one coming to the throne of God correct posture. Your petition is sent with the results already in your hand. Humbly draw near to God. Not just for Him to listen to a monologue but to engage in a dialogue with Him. Showing The Father that you are there for Him and not just your requests. Go in knowing that His will has already been done. Now you're ready to walk through it.

Jesus not only instructs the disciples on how to pray but also prays for the them. We see this in John 17:1-19 (NLT);

> "After saying all these things,
> Jesus looked up to heaven and
> said, "Father, the hour has come.
> Glorify your Son so he can give
> glory back to you. (2.) For you have

given him authority over everyone.
He gives eternal life to each one
you have given him. (3.) And this
is the way to have eternal life—to
know you, the only true God, and
Jesus Christ, the one you sent
to earth. (4.) I brought glory to
you here on earth by completing
the work you gave me to do. (5.)
Now, Father, bring me into the
glory we shared before the world
began. (6.) "I have revealed you to
the ones you gave me from this
world. They were always yours.
You gave them to me, and they
have kept your word. (7.) Now
they know that everything I have
is a gift from you, (8.) for I have
passed on to them the message
you gave me. They accepted it
and know that I came from you,
and they believe you sent me. (9.)
"My prayer is not for the world,
but for those you have given me,

because they belong to you. (10.)
All who are mine belong to you,
and you have given them to me,
so they bring me glory. (11.) Now
I am departing from the world;
they are staying in this world, but
I am coming to you. Holy Father,
you have given me your name;
now protect them by the power
of your name so that they will be
united just as we are. (12.) During
my time here, I protected them by
the power of the name you gave
me. I guarded them so that not one
was lost, except the one headed
for destruction, as the Scriptures
foretold. (13.) "Now I am coming
to you. I told them many things
while I was with them in this
world so they would be filled with
my joy. (14.) I have given them your
word. And the world hates them
because they do not belong to the
world, just as I do not belong to

the world. (15.) I'm not asking you
to take them out of the world, but
to keep them safe from the evil
one. (16.) They do not belong to
this world any more than I do. (17.)
Make them holy by your truth;
teach them your word, which is
truth. (18.) Just as you sent me into
the world, I am sending them into
the world. (19.) And I give myself
as a holy sacrifice for them so they
can be made holy by your truth."

In this particular partition of prayer he even
prayed for us. For you, in your now! He also prays
for all generations to come. We find this in John
17:20-26 (NLT);

""I am praying not only for these
disciples but also for all who will
ever believe in me through their
message (21.) I pray that they will
all be one, just as you and I are
one—as you are in me, Father, and
I am in you. And may they be in us

so that the world will believe you
sent me. (22.) "I have given them
the glory you gave me, so they
may be one as we are one. (23.)
I am in them and you are in me.
May they experience such perfect
unity that the world will know
that you sent me and that you love
them as much as you love me.
(24.) Father, I want these whom
you have given me to be with me
where I am. Then they can see all
the glory you gave me because you
loved me even before the world
began! (25.) "O righteous Father,
the world doesn't know you, but I
do; and these disciples know you
sent me. (26.) I have revealed you
to them, and I will continue to do
so. Then your love for me will be
in them, and I will be in them.""

Conversations with The Father were not
casual for Jesus. Prayer was and is Jesus' Culture.

He still intercedes on our behalf at the right hand of God. He literally gave his life for you! He was raised and is living for you! He continues pleading for you! He is forever praying for you! We find this in Romans 8:34 (NLT);

> "Who then will condemn us? No
> one—for Christ Jesus died for us
> and was raised to life for us, and
> he is sitting in the place of honor at
> God's right hand, pleading for us."

Jesus has reached the time that He foreknew He was approaching. He is aware that he will soon begin the final steps in his process to fulfill his God given assignment. What is His response? To PRAY. Understand that our inward encounters, by way of prayer, lead to our outward experiences.

He goes to the garden of Gethsemane to pray. He is accompanied and yet secluded. He is alone and distressed by what is to come. Mark 14:35-36 (NLT);

> "He went on a little farther and
> fell to the ground. He prayed that,
> if it were possible, the awful hour

awaiting him might pass him by.
(36.) "Abba, Father," he cried out,
"everything is possible for you.
Please take this cup of suffering
away from me. Yet I want your
will to be done, not mine.""

He is in anguish but decides that he will press in and go a little further. He resolves, "yet I want Your will to be done, not mine". This affirmation exhibits how essential it is for us to go farther! Press into what The Lord wills you to do.

LEVEL UP

NOTES

_____

_____

_____

_____

_____

_____

_____

_____

_____

_____

_____

_____

_____

_____

_____

_____

_____

_____

_____

_____

LEVEL 4

Jesus Is Arrested

Jesus knows of the nearing betrayal. He is even aware as to who it is. He loves him anyway. He feeds him, washes his feet and encourages him to "Do it quickly". John 13:27 (NLT);

"When Judas had eaten the
bread, Satan entered into him.
Then Jesus told him, "Hurry and
do what you're going to do.""

Jesus, being divine, is cognizant of God's timeline. The moment has met it. He is mindful of Judas' disloyalty but this characteristic is necessary to redeem the written word. Now the time has come. We read this in John 18:4-8 (NLT);

> "Jesus fully realized all that was going to happen to him, so he stepped forward to meet them. "Who are you looking for?" he asked. (5.) "Jesus the Nazarene," they replied. "I AM he," Jesus said. (Judas, who betrayed him, was standing with them.) (6.) As Jesus said "I AM he," they all drew back and fell to the ground! (7.) Once more he asked them, "Who are you looking for?" And again they replied, "Jesus the Nazarene." (8.) "I told you that I AM he," Jesus said. "And since I am the one you want, let these others go.""

Jesus boldly comes forward. He is courageously armed with the peace of Jehovah

Shalom. The presence of the Holy Spirit, so heavily draped upon him, knocked the soldiers coming to get him to the ground (John 18:6). He dauntlessly steps forward girded with the grace of God, engulfed with the fullness of His design. He is ready.

LEVELS OF TRUST

Jesus is in a fortified state of mind. But the disciples, not so much. Simon Peter assumed the position of coming to his "defense". Peter is terrified, angry and heartbroken. Every teaching Jesus ever gave completely out of the window. He functions naturally. John 18:10 (NLT);

> "Then Simon Peter drew a sword
> and slashed off the right ear of
> Malchus, the high priest's slave."

Jesus dripping with The Glory of our Lord and unsurpassable peace sternly turns to remind him he still has more to learn. John 18:11 (NLT);

> "But Jesus said to Peter, "Put your
> sword back into its sheath. Shall I

not drink from the cup of suffering
the Father has given me?""

This demonstration teaches us how to uphold the commands of God with excellence. How to hold fast to every thing we've been taught and still be teachable. He even goes as far to say in Matthew 26:52-54 (NLT);

> ""Put away your sword," Jesus
> told him. "Those who use the
> sword will die by the sword. (53.)
> Don't you realize that I could
> ask my Father for thousands
> of angels to protect us, and he
> would send them instantly?
> (54.) But if I did, how would
> the Scriptures be fulfilled that
> describe what must happen now?""

Jesus operated in his authority, yet he never stepped out of his jurisdiction. He is actively and effectively walking in his full capacity as the Son.

LEVEL UP

NOTES

_____

_____

_____

_____

_____

_____

_____

_____

_____

_____

_____

_____

_____

_____

_____

_____

_____

_____

_____

_____

_____

_____

LEVEL 5

Jesus Forgives

Jesus was brutally tortured, stripped, beaten, spit on and chained. While being mocked, rejected, abused, utterly humiliated and made to carry his own cross. The very cross they grotesquely nailed him to, while they did it, he prayed for them. He prayed for us, you and me. For all of those ignorant to who he is, what he did and for what he is doing. This prayer was for all who rejected him, then and now. A prayer for those who choose to turn a blind eye toward his sacrifice.

In Luke 23:34 (NLT);

> "Jesus said, "Father, forgive them,
> for they don't know what they are
> doing." And the soldiers gambled
> for his clothes by throwing dice."

He stared into the face of perpetual sin and prays for ALL of mankind. Humanity of yesterday, today and humanity to come.

LEVELS OF TRUST

They displayed contempt. They hung a sign. They consistently requested proof. Unfortunately fourteen generations (over 2000 years) later not much has changed. People may not be at the foot of the cross but instead express the same attitudes on the altar of their hearts. Jesus knew there would be some, but not all. Not once does he say anything to them. There is no inclination to prove himself in this moment. But a promise was made to the thief that hung next to him. To the one who sees him now. One who possesses a heart of repentance. One with no scales over their eyes. One with the fear of The Lord resting on the mantle of their heart. To the one who recognizes Jesus. Jesus recognizes the one.

LEVEL UP

NOTES

_____

_____

_____

_____

_____

_____

_____

_____

_____

_____

_____

_____

_____

_____

_____

_____

_____

_____

_____

_____

_____

_____

LEVEL 6

Jesus Fights Abandonment

This is the hour of great mercy. It may seem ironic, being that this is the hour Jesus cries out in disparity. We read this in Matthew 27:46 (NLT);

> "At about three o'clock, Jesus called out with a loud voice, "Eli, Eli, lema sabachthani?" which

means "My God, my God, why
have you abandoned me?""

It is 3 o'clock. The sixth hour to the ninth hour restoration was occurring. Jesus was literally restoring the connection between man and God. In that time the ninth hour (3pm) was the fixed time of prayer. It is before sunset when a new day would begin. It is all significant. There would not be another day without God's presence.

In this moment Jesus is anchored in our human nature. Normality, as it was known, is shaken up. He shouts to God twice. Once for God The Father. Twice for the Holy Spirit. Only one "Thou" which acknowledges that they are One. The God Head. The third Man in agony and darkness. Jesus lived in the abundance of God's presence in LIGHT, LIFE and LOVE. It was abnormal for him to not be encompassed by it. He is thrusted into sin and death, in an instant He has taken our place.

LEVELS OF TRUST

He continued to surrender even though he didn't feel God. Jesus knew he must go forward. In spite of the overwhelming typhoon of emotions that seemed to fill the void of God's presence, he remained. He consented to God's perfect will by staying steadfast in the work. He made the conscious decision of staying engaged and committed to this portion of the assignment. His abandonment was felt, it was legitimate. God will not behold sin. Habakkuk 1:13a (NLT);

> "But You are pure and cannot
> stand the sight of evil."

The Father thoroughly yielded to himself. He gives way to His will of reconciliation of God and man. "Abandoning" Jesus was God giving His self over, being wholly free from restraint of His own hand. Inevitably allowing Him to have His own way. In this God completed His own word. It was the foundation laid. God was there. He just didn't raise His hand to change it. God didn't stop it, He moved through it. This is a visual guide for us to see. Look to Him, the One who still moves, even when you feel stuck. The assignment may be painstaking and excruciating but we must die to get to the new place. To get to the next place.

Jesus exhibited the fight it takes to release the Spirit of God into the earth. His prayer was a whole hearted petition. It exposed the real place. It was an unveiling of how we need to pray from this place. The real place of where we are. The place of the fight as well as the place of yielding. In one sentence this prayer demonstrated;

1. Exhortation: Language intended to provoke in purpose. Intended for man to turn.
2. Illustration: To show by example. Demonstration. Illuminating the path to reach the goal.
3. Application: Putting it all to use. Administering one thing onto another with great effort, care and persistence.

Because of Jesus' prayer and determination to finish his course we have been reconciled. We are free indeed. Absolutely free to receive salvation and triumph. Now God can see you and not just your sin.

LEVEL UP

NOTES

LEVEL 7

Jesus Entrusts His Spirit

We are back to the beginning of this book. Understand going back to the beginning can be extremely beneficial. Sometimes we're ready to just jump to the end of a thing but it's crucial to see what it takes to get there.

It is now time for the last and final stretch of Jesus' journey. His mission here is almost completed. Each step closer to destiny became more challenging. But commending each step to God made every step possible, no matter how arduous! Shadowing Jesus, the living example, we must give it ALL to The Father. Luke 23:46 (NLT);

"Then Jesus shouted, "Father,
I entrust my spirit into your
hands!" And with those words
he breathed his last."

Every "end" holds a new beginning, another level. The closer you get to your next the further it may feel. Keep going! It is vital to go a little further. To continue or even create that ripple. INTERCEDE. PERSEVERE. OVERCOME. Someone needed to witness Jesus's every step. Someone needs to witness yours. Watching you go from darkness into the marvelous light. Witnessing that progression is available. Seeing The Truth is proof that the goal is tangible.

Placing every trial, situation and obstacle into the strong right hand of God gave Jesus a fresh wind. For the next level, a fresh oil. For the next trust, a fresh anointing.

At every level of trust Jesus' capacity grew and matured. Entrusting our journey, along with every aspect of our lives, enables our capacity to grow. It enables every facet of our life to mature. In doing this we will gain the capacity to grow in love, power and authority. We will acquire the capacity to be developed back into God's image. Shake off natural fact and grab a hold to spiritual truth.

We have to truly learn how to die to self every day. How to entrust every one of our levels. How to depend on the Triune Deliverer. In doing these things we will confidently be able to commend our entire being into The Father's hands. Only then will we undeniably live FOR REAL!!!

LEVEL UP

NOTES

_____

_____

_____

_____

_____

_____

_____

_____

_____

_____

_____

_____

_____

_____

_____

_____

_____

_____

_____

_____

_____

_____

Printed in the United States
by Baker & Taylor Publisher Services